Tiff and the Big Top

By Sascha Goddard

"Tiff, the Big Top is here," said Nan.

"We can go and have fun!"

But Tiff was in a huff.

Tiff was gruff at Nan.

"The Big Top is **not** fun," said Tiff.

"I can see lots of fun stuff!"
said Nan.

Nan set off up the hill.

"I can not see fun stuff," said Tiff.

But Tiff ran up the hill.

"Do not huff and puff, Tiff," said Nan.

"Look up! It's fab!"

Tiff did look up at
the Big Top.

It **was** fab!

"See, Tiff?" said Nan.
"There is fun stuff at
the Big Top."

"It **is** fun at the Big Top!"
said Tiff.

CHECKING FOR MEANING

1. Why did Nan want to go to the Big Top? *(Literal)*

2. How did Tiff feel about going to the Big Top? *(Literal)*

3. Do you think Nan was right to encourage Tiff to go to the Big Top? Why? *(Inferential)*

EXTENDING VOCABULARY

here	Where is *here*? Is it close or a long way away? What is another word that sounds the same, but is written using different letters? I.e. hear. What does this word mean? What do you use to hear?
gruff	What does *gruff* mean? What are some other words you know that have a similar meaning? E.g. annoyed, stern, angry, grumpy, bad-tempered.
stuff	What is the meaning of this word in the story? Can you use this word in different sentences to show that it has another meaning? E.g. I put my *stuff* in my bag.

MOVING BEYOND THE TEXT

1. What is another name for a Big Top?

2. If you could do an activity that happens at a Big Top, what would it be? Why?

3. What equipment is needed to move Big Tops from one place to another?

4. Where do the people who perform live when they are travelling from place to place?

SPEED SOUNDS

| ff | ll | ss | zz |

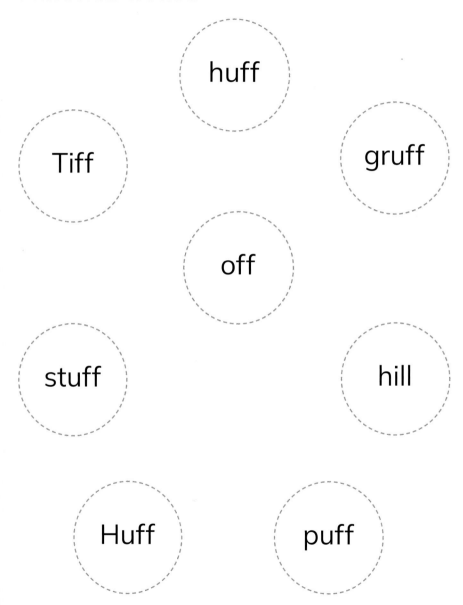

huff

Tiff

gruff

off

stuff

hill

Huff

puff